The Cornish Countryside

SARAH FOOT

BOSSINEY BOOKS

First published in 1983
by Bossiney Books
St Teath, Bodmin, Cornwall.
Designed, printed and bound in Great Britain by
A. Wheaton & Co, Exeter.

*For my daughter Camilla
who knows and loves
the Cornish Countryside
as well as I do*

Plate Acknowledgments

Cover photography of Roche Rock and Cotehele Quay
by Ray Bishop
Pages 4–6 upper, 9, 11–13, 15–20 upper, 21, 24–27,
32, 33, 42, 43, 46–55, 64, 65, 70 lower, 71, 77–85, 89, 92,
93, 96, 98–103, 105, 106, 107 lower, 109, 112, 114, 115
Ray Bishop
Pages 3, 6 lower, 7, 8, 10, 14, 20 lower, 22, 23, 34, 39, 41,
44, 56–61, 67, 70 upper, 72–75, 104, 107 upper, 113, 116,
117 Alice Lennox-Boyd
Pages 29–31, 36–38, 45, 66, 68, 69, 108 Mike Frost
Pages 109, 110, 111 Edward Lennox-Boyd
Page 40 Royal Institution of Cornwall
Page 63 S. Bennetts
Page 87 Robert Roskrow
Page 90 Royal Cornwall Show
Page 91 The Western Morning News
Pages 94, 95 J.C.M. Davidson
Page 97 Southgate Studio
Page 119 Neil Cradick

The Author and Publisher would like to thank William Collins Sons & Co. for permission to quote from
Bird Life in Cornwall by B. H. Ryves

ABOUT THE AUTHOR
AND THE BOOK

Sarah Foot lives at St Mellion, near Callington. Formerly on the staff of *The London Evening News*, she contributes regularly to *The Western Morning News*. This is her seventh title for Bossiney. In 1981 she wrote the text for *Views of Old Cornwall*, a collection of Victorian and Edwardian picture postcards, and followed it with *Views of Old Plymouth* in the Spring of 1983. Her other Bossiney titles are *A Cornish Camera*, in collaboration with photographer George Ellis, *My Grandfather Isaac Foot*, which was the subject of BBC TV tie-in, *Following the Tamar*, and *Following the River Fowey*.

Here in the first Bossiney publication to contain a combination of colour and black and white photography, Sarah Foot explores *The Cornish Countryside*. Words and photographs unite in presenting a beautifully evocative portrait of rich and varied landscapes. Moreover it is a living portrait, for Sarah Foot has travelled from one end of Cornwall to the other, meeting and talking with people who live and work in the countryside. 'I have visited many farms, talked to all sorts of people involved with the land from blacksmiths to sheep shearers and farm labourers who remember still the days of working with horses as the happiest of their lives.'

This book, a valuable addition to the Westcountry Library, comes from an author who loves and understands Cornwall, pinning people and places to paper with skill and sensitivity. 'The Spirit of Cornwall,' she writes, 'appeals to both strangers and those who belong. Almost indefinable, it is ever present. Stark and true, pagan and holy, often making beauty out of a scarred and mutilated earth, it is almost a contradiction in terms.'

The Cornish Countryside

The Cornish Countryside is the most underestimated slice of the whole county. The very word Cornwall brings to mind pictures of beaches, cliffs and marvellous seascapes. But there is so much more. Tucked away in winding lanes and folds of hidden fields and valleys lies some of the most beautiful countryside. It is less known than the well-trodden routes to the sea and beaches, but just as outstanding. Although one is always conscious of the proximity of the sea in this narrow toe of Britain, it is well worth venturing further inland.

Part of Cornwall's charm is that it avoids neat and easy classification: on one hand mining districts, many of them now forgotten and derelict; on the other farmland sometimes with almost impossibly steep fields clinging to valley sides, the rivers providing a backdrop to many a Cornish scene. On this exploration of the Cornish countryside I have often found

'Tucked away in winding lanes and
folds of hidden fields lies some of the
most beautiful countryside.'
Right: Pont in the Fowey Valley.
Left: Bodmin Moor.

myself close to water and sometimes on it.

Though the valleys of Cornwall draw me back again and again, her moorland is just as remarkable. Not lush and kind and giving, but gaunt and strong, timeless and full of varying atmosphere. People either love Cornwall or feel rejected by it. There does not seem room for those who do not fall under the spell of this rare and independent land.

Each year I think I have found the place I love the most. When I was a child it was the banks of the Lynher River; later I fell for the Fowey valley. But more recently I have returned with a kind of hunger again and again to that flinty land beyond St Just. Mine houses built into treacherous cliffs; tiny stone cot-

'Cornwall would not be Cornwall without the stone monuments and strange granite edifices.' Duloe stone circle, one of many archaeological treasures to be found in the county.

tages attached to small granite fields cultivated by miners and fishermen to supplement their meagre living. Even the light seems more dramatic there as it glances off the treeless landscape turning rocks and boulders from silver grey to mellow gold.

Many men and women who have made their living off the land in Cornwall have done it on a very small scale, using to the best advantage a few acres. There are market gardeners, flower growers, farmers, and embellishing it all, the men who built, and happily still do, the Cornish hedges with their carefully structured stone walls.

I have visited many farms, talked to all sorts of people involved with the land from blacksmiths to sheep shearers to farm labourers who remember still the days of working with horses as the happiest of their lives. I have listened and watched people who have tried to keep many of the old customs going.

Cornwall would not be Cornwall without the great

Left: 'Mine houses built into the treacherous cliff' at Botallack near St Just. Right: On the Lynher River at the other end of the county.

stone monuments and strange granite edifices. Likewise, it would not be the same without the lushly growing hedges thick with ferns and campion, primroses and bluebells, hundreds of wild flowers of every variety. This is not the land of wide open spaces but rather views that are glimpsed from time to time between steeply rising hills, in dips and round bends, over hedges or framed in gateways.

Churches are an integral part of the landscape, as are the stark and simple chapels that came later with the Methodists. Unless you understand the great effect the Wesleys and their new form of worship had upon the mining, farming and fishing folk in the eighteenth century, you will not understand the feeling that still runs through the Cornish countryside.

The landscape has also been shaped by what has been dug and hewn from under the earth: great granite and slate quarries now left in silence with their huge slabs of stone and bottomless watery pools reflecting the chiselled walls around: the white peaks of the china-clay district, a weird and compelling moonscape; mine buildings strewn across moorland, valley and cliff—strangely thrilling though they borrow their beauty from a sad and gruelling past that cost many a man his life.

Jack Clemo, the Cornish writer and poet who has been blind and deaf for most of his life, lives and writes in the china-clay mining district. He has proved once and for all that the Cornish countryside is much more about the way you feel than what you see. It is a sensation as well as a sight:

> Sour clay faces slunk from the dream;
> Ascetic contours rasped through summer haze
> Beyond the lithe corn and the poppies' blaze.
> Where the unmined valley
> Closed·in on a nudging stream,
> A few stacks loomed tall and obstinate
> Beside the hidden furnace, near a field gate.

Since time immemorial Cornish people have created strange buildings from the rocks that abound. Out of the great grey rocks at Roche a hermit of the fifteenth century built a chapel, carrying vast chunks

Above: '... the lushly growing hedges thick with primroses.'
Right: '... the white peaks of the china-clay district, a weird and compelling moonscape.'

Above: The Minack Theatre on the cliff at Porthcurno. Celtic designs embellish the tiers of concrete seats set among the natural granite.   Left: 'Churches are an integral part of the landscape.' Here the Church at St Just in Roseland hugs the river bank.

of granite to the top in a task that seems almost beyond man's capabilities.

Rowena Cade kept this tradition alive. In 1929 she was the master mind behind the Minack Theatre, a wide open stage built amongst the rocks on the cliff at Porthcurno. Much of the manual work she performed herself embellishing concrete with Celtic designs and crosses to blend with the stone. Shakespeare's *Tempest* was the first play performed there in the natural amphitheatre. It was the success of this production that inspired Miss Cade to build the theatre which has now become world famous and remains as a memorial to a remarkable woman who died in 1983.

'Trees do not stand straight but have been sculpted and misshapen by fierce winds.'

Gwennap Pit, 'Cornwall's most famous amphitheatre ...
where John Wesley once preached to 20,000 followers.'

'One is always conscious of the
sea in this narrow toe of Britain...'

Cornwall's most famous amphitheatre is Gwennap Pit where John Wesley once preached to 20,000 followers and where today, more than two hundred years later, Methodists still have a great reunion at Whitsun. That this dip in the ground was formed by mining subsidence seems somehow most appropriate.

Then there are the Round Houses at Veryan with their thatched roofs topped with crosses. Built in this shape to keep the devil out, they say, they were the inspiration of a caring vicar of the nineteenth century,

A Round House at Veryan — 'Built in this shape to keep the devil out,' they say.

Jeremiah Twist, who was worried about accommodation for his flock. That tradition has been continued by the behest of Maria Kempe Homeyard. In the 1940s it was her wish that two more round houses be built at Veryan with the stipulation that they should preferably house widows of Cornish seamen.

I have to stress that this is a very personal, very selective expedition through the Cornish countryside. To have written on all the facets of the landscape would have needed 100,000 words and many, many more pictures. But I hope in this book I have managed to capture some of the spirit of Cornwall. It is a spirit that has appealed both to strangers and those who belong. Almost indefinable, it is ever present. Stark and true, pagan and holy, often making beauty out of a scarred and mutilated earth it is almost a contradiction in terms. The greatest insult is to oversentimentalise the place. If you are looking for gentleness you will find it only in the air; if you seek sunshine you will often find rain. Trees do not stand straight but have been sculpted and misshapen by fierce winds.

Everywhere there is mystery and legend in the landscape and an intermingling of past and present. I defy any Cornishman or lover of Cornwall to go to Land's End, however many tourists may be there, and not to be sure, yet again, that there lies the Lost Land of Lyonesse. Cornish fairy stories are fact not fiction and often they have tragic endings.

Thomas Hardy came in search of the elusive spirit of Cornwall, and many years later he wrote:

> When I came back from Lyonesse
> With magic in my eyes,
> All marked with mute surprise
> My radiance rare and fathomless,
> When I came back from Lyonesse
> With magic in my eyes.

I can only hope that this collection of words and pictures will evoke some of that 'radiance rare and fathomless' conjured up by the Cornish countryside which has bewitched so many over the years.

The Author at Land's End.

14

Bodmin Moor

Bodmin Moor is the heart of Cornwall. I go there when my batteries need recharging and always return feeling invigorated by the experience. Whether I am visiting the farm of a friend, walking across to Brown Willy, the highest point on the moor, gazing at the great structures of stone such as the Cheesewring and Trethevy Quoit or seeing the engine houses of the old mines etched against the horizon, I never fail to be excited by this underestimated moorland.

Life on Bodmin Moor has never been easy and only a special sort of person can withstand the weather and the gaunt atmosphere of the unprotected land mass. But it has a beauty of its own which I have never found bettered, though some people consider it too stark and barren to give them such pleasure.

I have been caught in the swiftly falling mists and know how frightening and disorientating they can be. Once I walked to the source of the River Fowey when there were still huge snowdrifts around and saw the landscape transformed. I have been there on balmy spring and summer days when clouds cast purple shadows across heather and bracken. The rounded shapes of the hills and valleys seemed to wallow in the mellow sun.

'Bodmin Moor is the heart of Cornwall ... gaunt and strong, timeless and full of varying atmosphere.'
Left: the Cheesewring near Minions.
Right: Roughtor with the memorial to Charlotte Dymond in the foreground, the lass who was murdered by her lover at this spot in 1844.

Dozmary Pool where legend says King Arthur threw his sword Excalibur when he was dying.

Dozmary Pool is one of my favourite places and I have experienced in all seasons the strange, almost ghostly, atmosphere. Legend says this is the lake into which King Arthur threw his sword Excalibur as he lay dying and to be near that unexplained saucer-like lake in the middle of the moor is to believe such legendary tales without any difficulty.

I have known for some years a woman farmer on the moor. Ann Hunt has seventy acres of fenced land and runs sheep up on several hundred acres of common moorland. She has been there for six years and has developed a real sense of belonging. She says she has never known anything but helpfulness from her fellow farmers who have all grown to accept her.

I have been with her to Liskeard market, still the main meeting place for farmers in the area, and watched her as she talked to her neighbours and fellow farmers; she will ask easily for advice and they come to her, too, already treating her as an equal. There is a camaraderie amongst the people who live and work on the moor that forms a special brotherhood of its own.

One morning I watched her high up on the moor as her dog Sweep helped her round up the sheep. His actions are so quick, his obedience so instant, that Ann says he is worth several pairs of human hands. It is always thrilling to see a dog and its master working closely together. Ann's dog watches her all the time, sometimes almost anticipating her next word of command, then darting off to perform his task with willingness and evident pleasure.

She has harsh words, though, for people who wander the moors with untrained dogs which often get in among her sheep. There is nothing that will make her angrier than to find a new born lamb mauled by an unattended dog.

King Arthur's Downs with Roughtor and Brown Willy, the highest point in Cornwall, in the background.

Granite is almost a symbol of Cornwall — stones of every kind people the Moor, natural outcrops or hewn by man and placed to serve some purpose over the ages.

One of the Moor's many clapper bridges — this one is near St Breward.

The sheep on the moor lamb later than those kept on lower pastures and one late spring day when the sky was blue, the light razor sharp and the whole moorland at its most appealing, I went with Ann to check her lambing ewes. As we arrived it was obvious that a birth was imminent but there was some difficulty. With expert hands Ann helped that little lamb into the world.

Above us a skylark hovered singing its bright clear song; beyond stood the stone backdrop of the Cheesewring and the Silver Valley engine house. We were enclosed in that flinty granite land and it felt for a moment that all life that mattered existed there in that perfect moment of birth in those almost painfully beautiful surroundings.

We did not speak. Words would have been irrelevant and inadequate. I thought myself that Ann must experience all this so many times it cannot mean the same to her. But she looked up and smiled and I knew she felt it too: that knowledge that this was a particular moment to be frozen in the memory for ever after.

When Ann's sheep wander off the moor into

Ann Hunt counts her sheep on the Moor. She runs sheep on several hundred acres of common moorland.

neighbours' fields, relationships are good so there are no recriminations, and she is quick to get out horse and dog to drive them back to their moorland territory and away from the deadly roads.

After five years, in 1982, she was confident enough to select her own rams and I drove with her to the other side of the moor to collect those she had chosen. We bundled them into the back of the landrover and went home triumphant. Whenever I have watched her with animals I have envied her the strength she has and noticed her true farmer's attitude to animals; no time for sentimentality, but treat them well for they are your livelihood.

Ann makes good use of her farm produce and to have a meal at her farmhouse, Hendrifton, is an experience never to be forgotten. Everything at the large table in front of the huge open fireplace has been produced on the farm. She makes her own butter and cream and bread. And in the corner of the sitting room stands her spinning wheel on which she spins her own wool and later knits it into chunky jerseys to keep out the moorland winter winds.

Once a year, on Boxing Day, the Hunts have open house for the evening and all the neighbours for miles around come to eat, drink and make merry—all the people she has relied on throughout the year, people who have helped her out in emergencies, lent her machinery, helped her to mend fences, given her good advice. There is a mixed group of ages and types and occupations drawn together in the brotherhood of the moor. Later in the evening there is a singsong of Cornish songs collected over the years by Ann and her husband.

Ann Hunt has two neighbours of whom she is particularly fond. Both very different characters, Joe Halls and Malcolm Oliver.

Joe Halls is one of Bodmin Moor's most famous farmers. He's been on the moor since he was a boy and

now owns nearly 1,000 acres of moorland. He lives in unchanged Carkeet House, slate faced and granite pillared. Below the house runs the River Fowey. His son Peter farms on the other side of the valley.

For years he rounded up his cattle on horseback, never owned a car and lived without electricity. Even now he only has candlelight and does not bother to trim the lamps which once lit the house when the family lived there.

He is a man of his word and was respected for that and his knowledge of livestock. He now only potters

Foxgloves on the Moor, a haven for wildlife as well as numerous species of flowers. 'I never fail to be excited by this underestimated moorland.'

about doing essential jobs for he is eighty one years old. He meant to move to Darite where he built a bungalow for himself and his wife to retire to, but when the time came he could not face leaving the moor. His wife could no longer endure the hard life but she visits him regularly and he goes down to Darite to see her sometimes bearing peat for the fire which he has dug from his land for years. 'It smells so sweet,' he told me.

He is full of strong views on almost any subject and once he starts a conversation I am held in rapture. His voice is still strong and rises and falls with his thick Cornish accent and he uses many words which are no longer generally heard.

Ann shearing sheep at her farm, Hendrifton (above right). She spins and knits her own wool and makes her own butter and cream.

He is a staunch Methodist, as so many of the original moorland farmers were, and he can remember walking to St Luke's Chapel near Bolventor. There was a time when most families on this part of the moor would walk to chapel once, or even twice, on a Sunday. 'You could see the lights they carried glinting in the distance as they walked in the darkness to the evening service.'

These habits have nearly died out and the wonderful celebrations on Sunday School anniversaries are only a shadow of the past when the organ was carried outside and everyone gathered to sing those Wesleyan hymns with fervent voices.

Every time I go to visit Joe Halls he greets me with a warm welcome and entertains me with fresh home-baked bread and his own butter and cream. He sits by the Rayburn with his feet up and talks away about any subject you care to mention. He is not narrow-minded or blinkered in his way of life. From his high and rough moorland site he seems to have viewed all of life's problems and joys and seen it with a particular kind of originality and generosity so that he finds it hard to judge another man unless he is dishonest.

I have never met a man who so belongs to the place where he lives; who, quite simply, could not survive if he was not there. He would never tell you he loves it; he will tell you of all the hardships and discomforts of living there, but he will not, cannot, leave it.

Another of Ann's neighbours is Malcolm Oliver. He

Though Malcolm Oliver still enjoys his work and is out and about on the farm from dawn until dusk he says nothing can replace the excitement of his early farming days at East Taphouse. 'The first calves I had born made for some of the happiest times in my life, each one was as if it was a miracle. But now in a busy week we sometimes have ten or fifteen calves born on this farm. It isn't the same thing as it was in those early days when I was just beginning.'

He farms his 320 acres by doing 'everything that the books tell you not to do. We don't specialise in anything but do old-fashioned mixed farming with dairy, beef, sheep and corn. We don't make a fortune but we live very well and we are happy. What more can a family want?' Mr Oliver thinks that too many people hanker after too much and the result is that they are never happy.

Malcolm Oliver was prepared for his children wanting to go away and find work elsewhere but all his daughters decided to stay on the farm. Wendy burst into tears when she did so well in her exams and her father tried to persuade her to move on. She thought he did not want her to stay, but of course he did and was delighted when she took over management of the cows. Now Wendy is married to Joe Hall's

Joe Halls, now over eighty, is one of Bodmin Moor's most famous farmers. On the Moor since he was a boy, he lives at Carkeet House (right).

started his farming life looking after twenty seven acres at East Taphouse. Now he owns over 300 acres at Rosecraddoc. He has the same longing to leave the results of his hard work and accomplishments to his family and is not a bit deterred that he has five daughters and no sons.

All his daughters have worked on the farm, each with their own responsibility, and when I visited them at their large farmhouse I saw the same bond created by a family working together that I have seen before in large Cornish farming families.

The Moor shields many a steep valley. Here (above) Gam Bridge crosses the River Camel. Left: The Old Inn at St Breward, one of Cornwall's highest hostelries. Right: Brown Willy from Roughtor.

*King Arthur's Hall, an earthwork built by early inhabi-
tants of the Moor — nobody knows for what purpose.*

grandson and so the tapestry of the moorland families becomes further involved. The other daughters all play their part too. Lynne drives the tractor, sees to the cultivation and the sheep; Sonia once married took over the indoor jobs and book-keeping; Allison works with the pigs and Rosalind is general manager of the stock and goes to market.

I sat one morning in their large farmhouse kitchen while the small grandchildren played in their play-pen. The girls came in to join their mother for a mid-morning cup of coffee. It seemed remarkable to see a family working together happily at a time when many families are split and we are constantly being told that the generation gap causes so many differences.

At his second farm, Tremelleck, Malcolm Oliver has been indulging one of his hobbies. He has been doing up for holiday cottages two of the farm buildings which were once in danger of collapse. He is determined that the cottages should look as similar to their

*The Commoners have the right to run stock on the Moor
— not only sheep and cattle but horses and even donkeys.*

original state as possible so he collects and then spends hours selecting each stone for the walls in order that they will fit and match and correspond as nearly as possible to the old stone walls built a hundred years ago.

Many old farm buildings have been left to decay because it is not financially viable to repair them, so it was a real thrill to see a farmer finding a way of preserving part of our heritage.

Many of the farmers I have spoken to or known throughout Cornwall have worked hard and acquired expertise and land from very humble beginnings, often starting as tenant farmers on other people's land.

They all seem to have one objective in mind, that their families should benefit in some way, and it is remarkable how many of these farmers have at least one offspring who wants to follow in their footsteps. For Joe Halls and Malcolm Oliver this is obviously all the reward they need.

Nature Conservation in Cornwall

It was one of the nicest invitations I ever had and it came so unexpectedly. One day someone appeared at my door and introduced herself as Amy Maunder. She said she was a farmer's wife from nearby in the Tamar valley and would I like to go and visit her to see some kestrels which had nested in her barn.

For some years now, the Maunders have had this annual treat of watching kestrels nest and hatch out in a large barn just behind their house. I was greatly honoured to be invited to visit them and see the birds for the Maunders guard them jealously knowing that sometimes indiscriminate and uncaring people can frighten them away.

Mrs Maunder and I walked one glowing yellow-lit summer evening across the meadow opposite their farmhouse. Into the sweet smelling barn we went, up the sturdy ladder and then across the top of the barn amongst the straw bales. Then we saw them, four baby kestrels, only three or four weeks old and sitting by an open window. They were gazing from their vantage point seemingly awaiting their mother who had gone hunting. Around them lay the down of their early days, now discarded.

As we sat snugly amongst the hay and talked quietly between ourselves I could see that the birds were not frightened, as if they knew and trusted their landlady, for Amy Maunder visits them every day to see how they are doing and sits and watches them for hours.

Their sharp little beaks were already fashioned for hunting and their haunting eyes were already all-knowing and all-seeing; they never took their gaze from us slightly suspicious and curious.

I have never been so close to such newly-born kestrels—all we needed to do was stretch out our hands and we could have touched them—but all the while we felt that this was their home, that we were the guests there on sufferance.

I don't know how long we sat there watching and talking, noting the marking clear and crossed on their back and wings, knowing they would one day fly to kill, dominate a world of dangerous living. All I do know was that I was aware that it was a perfect time, one that was full of wonder and would be remembered ever after. Mrs Maunder's soft voice, the watchfulness and dominance of the birds, the comfort of our seats among the hay and straw and the smell and atmosphere of the great old barn which must have seen so much in its lifetime, all moulded together to make me feel as if I was in a secret newly-discovered world. Like a child who is somewhere it is not usually allowed but which has been sanctioned just this once.

Outside, as we walked away, Mrs Maunder told me how the barn owls and little owls had also nested there and how she had watched them grow, eat and learn to fly. She had watched the kestrels over several years and often wondered whether it was the same kestrels who returned once grown-up to make their nests and have their families in their turn. She has watched the mother kestrel come and strip the meat fine for her

'I have never been so close to such newly-born kestrels —
all we needed to do was stretch out our hands and we could
have touched them — but all the while we felt that this
was their home, that we were the guests there on
sufferance.'

Hooked beak and claws are the hallmark of the bird of prey. Once classed as vermin, these elegant birds are now treasured on the wildlife scene. The buzzard chicks below were born on Bodmin Moor in a nest only eight feet above ground. Both fledged successfully, no doubt to be seen perched on a roadside telegraph pole or soaring effortlessly high above the countryside, their mewing cry betraying their identity.

The ghostly form of the Barn owl hunting along the hedgerows is sadly on the decline due to demolition of many old barns and farmhouses. At this nest site in an old Cornish stone barn, the adult owls had caught and laid eleven mice in a row beside the chicks.
The Little owl (above left) is not indigenous to this country but was introduced last century. This one was photographed in East Cornwall. It is now widespread throughout England although scarce in the South West.

spread about the lawns and meadows and the stone walls? All I could know for sure was that I had spent an evening in perfect company and occupation and in a happy, beautiful place. In an otherwise crazy world everything suddenly seemed possible and blessed.

There was a time when people took the natural life of the country for granted. There it was and, if it went away, too bad. But perhaps one of the great achievements of this century is the growing responsibility towards nature conservancy.

Cornwall's wildlife was diminished when the famous chough died out. This black bird has a greeny tinge to its feathers, red beak and legs and an unusual flying pattern. Once the symbol of Cornwall, it meant a great deal to the Cornish people, but sadly there are no longer any choughs in the wild here, only imported ones in the bird sanctuaries at Padstow and Hayle.

B.H. Ryves wrote in his *Bird Life of Cornwall 1948* the following passage about choughs which serves as a reminder of what we now miss.

'This elegant and charming bird is a member of the Corvidae family, one of the seven species of crows which are regular residents in the British Isles. Except that it is black, I can find little in it that resembles any crow. Its graceful form, its delightful manners and its whole way of life stamp it as well nigh unique among British birds.

'Its long curved red bill and red legs, its comely figure, its lively gait, its glossy blue-black plumage, tinged with green which glitters as it flashes through the sunlight, all these pronounce it a thoroughbred. Its clear ringing call, once its characteristic timbre is imprinted on the mind, can be mistaken for that of no other bird. In company with others of its kind it is at once playful and talkative, but never aggressive.

'The soaring of the chough I have witnessed only once, now many years ago. I do not include the normal

young; she has watched the father help too. She herself has had to help feed the young birds when the parents had for some reason gone missing. Over the years she has taken part and been accepted into a bird world that most people have never seen.

The slate-faced farmhouse and its beautiful garden had an almost hallowed feeling. Was this the goodness of the people who had lived there which was

spiral flights already described, not the circling aloft of a family of birds. I refer to true soaring. It was one of those perfect days that is sometimes vouchsafed to us in the month of May, with a cloudless sky and a soft zephyr wafted from a Southern clime. The cliff slopes were carpeted with wild hyacinths, pale yellow primroses and delicate fronds of infant bracken. It was surely a day and place that made life good to live. All the morning the choughs had been busy feeding their nestlings. Early in the afternoon, it seemed to me that the call of the vast liquid sky was irresistible to them. For one wonderful hour they just revelled in flight. Quitting the nest, they rose in great circles out over the open ocean, until they were lost to sight. It is pictures such as this that a man can treasure throughout life and indeed, their colouring is immortal.'

Reading that tract by B.H. Ryves makes me feel that we have lost part of life, but today there is still much that deserves preservation in Cornwall. Of course, many birds are now protected species, protected by the law, with the help of many concerned people, not least the Duke of Cornwall who has taken a keen interest in and around his Duchy land.

Barn owls, kestrels and the magnificent buzzards are all part of our country scene. I can sit in my garden and watch for hours the buzzards wheeling across the wooded hill opposite. Their grace, their magnificence never ceases to thrill me. Without them life would indeed be less colourful and joyful.

Watching the kestrels as they hover over a cornfield, who cannot be full of admiration at their timing and their judgment and their balance? When they swoop down there is no hope for their prey for they move so fast with such intent and singleness of purpose.

It is not only the bird life, but badgers and butterflies and all kinds of wild flowers that have to be protected in order that they may give future generations the amount of pleasure that they have given us and so that all these wild things both large and small may have the right to exist.

Primroses are among the first spring flowers to colonise the Cornish hedgerows.

Only yesterday I walked along a favourite ride of mine at the foot of the valley where I live. I was stopped in my tracks as a great winged heron rose just below me, swept quietly and effortlessly above and then, as if for my pleasure, wheeled in great circles until he disappeared downstream.

Within minutes, my heart still beating with excitement, a flash of the brightest colour caught my eye. It was a green woodpecker and he seemed like a darting arrow with his quick, no-nonsense flight. In through the trees he went until he perched on a vertical trunk as woodpeckers do. Was his nest there, I wondered? Was it his tap tapping I had heard early in the misty spring morning a few weeks before? A sound that always makes my heart quicken.

I turned to walk home, surprised at how much delight I had found in seeing both these birds at such close quarters, and, just as I thought there could be nothing more beautiful, two quacking shell ducks flew in front of me with the newly budding woods as background to their coupled flight. Had they laid their eggs in the ploughed field above as they had the year before?

Those three events in one April afternoon were enough to banish any sadness and to make one revel in Nature's beauty.

There are so many familiar sights in the countryside which we take for granted and which we would miss greatly if they were not there. The primroses and bluebells are part of our Cornish scenery and where would we be without the campion, the valerian and the exotic ferns? Once-common flowers like the cowslip have almost disappeared and yet previously they grew in many paddocks. A friend of mine gave me some from her garden which she had grown from seed taken from plants in her parents' garden and I am proud to say they are doing well and I like to think that I have done my bit to preserve them.

Philip Blamey has been chairman of the Cornwall Naturalists' Trust for seven years, in fact for a third of its lifetime. The name of the Trust is just about to be changed to the Cornwall Trust for Nature and Conservation, a name that is hoped will be more indicative of the work in which it is involved.

Mr Blamey considers that 'positive conservation in a modern context involves commonsense and talking to people early on with diplomacy'. He has been striving to do this for all the years he has been involved with the Trust which was started in 1962.

There are between 15,000 and 16,000 members and the Trust is working hard at the moment to extend their membership. Philip Blamey was once a farmer. Then he went into local politics and has helped his famous artist wife, Marjorie Blamey, with her writing and the planning of her best-seller books on wild flowers. He now writes books himself and is a man well equipped for his part in the Trust. 'I have worked closely with the County Council, planning committees, miners and oil men and have always found we could achieve much more by talking in the very early stages.'

The Trust is now responsible for seventeen nature reserves in Cornwall which involve over 2,000 acres: some reserves are leased; some are owned by other people and managed by the Trust; some have been given to the Trust; and some are owned freehold by the Trust. Many of these are Sights of Special Scientific Interest.

They have just acquired fifty acres of Red Moor which is their biggest and latest acquisition and all these reserves are a way of ensuring that much of the wildlife of Cornwall is preserved. The majority of them are open to the public. 'We believe in using nature reserves for education,' Mr Blamey told me. Many have special facilities so that wheel chairs can be taken there. The Church Town Field Studies Centre for the handicapped at Lanlivery use the facilities at Red Moor frequently.

At one of the Trust's reserves near Callington the land is owned by the Duchy of Cornwall, and Prince Charles, a keen conservationist and the Patron of the Royal Society for Nature Conservation, has visited the area with Philip Blamey and shown much interest. When he heard that the heath fritillary, a rare butterfly, was not breeding there as well as it did before the fir trees had been planted, he ordered the trees to be moved elsewhere. Four acres of new plantation had to be replanted 'elsewhere' and a few hundred trees felled. The trees had cut out the light and reduced the food plants and, since the fritillary is a lazy flier, they had diminished the butterflies' environment. In 1983 there have been over 1,000 fritillaries spotted in the area, whereas in 1981 there had only been fifty or sixty. 'I think it is too soon to say it was because of the removal of the trees; it was just one of those strange ways of nature,' Mr Blamey said.

Destruction of habitat and spraying with insecticides have resulted in the loss of many species of butterfly. In Cornwall sheltered valleys, sand dunes, cliffs and woods provide safe havens for these beautiful insects. Left: a small pearl-bordered fritillary. Right: Heath fritillaries mating.

After the primroses the bluebells add to the feast of colour.

The Cornwall Naturalists' Trust is surveying over 400 sites. '…sometimes just one rare plant is found in a hedge.'

Under a special Manpower Services scheme the Trust has been clearing and surveying over 400 sites of conservation interest. Sometimes just one rare plant is found in a hedge; it all counts as an important part of the Trust's work to preserve and place rare and wild flowers and plants.

'The hedge cutters are always getting the blame for everything, but do you know that all hedge cutters employed by the council go on a course that includes a section on conservation. Most of them are very good but since the best time to cut hedges is in August there is no way that all the hedges in the county can be cut in one month.'

Working in Cornwall Philip Blamey says that one is constantly aware that Nature is a wonderful reclaimer. After all, Red Moor is an industrial wasteland which has been turned into a rich nature reserve.

'Most of the destruction comes from man's greed,' Philip Blamey says. 'If you look at it from an aesthetic point of view wildlife has as much right to live as we do and it is man's responsibility to look after Nature.'

Having been a farmer, Philip Blamey sees that conservation must work alongside farming methods but he says that 'use of chemicals has been reduced greatly in recent times and agricultural herbicides are used more responsibly'.

There is an increasing interest throughout the world in conservation and Cornwall is fighting hard to retain the best habitats and most important species in its countryside. As has been proved in old mining areas, it is never too late to conserve parts of the country. In some of the most picturesque spots of today mine chimneys once belched smoke and mine waste seemingly ruined the countryside. And yet Nature has done her brilliant best and covered over such atrocities and left us with unforgettable landscapes which are somehow enhanced by the slight remaining scars caused by man's greed and disregard for natural wildlife.

The Most Westerly Point of Cornwall

When I drive down to the most westerly points of Cornwall, I feel I am visiting another world: the treeless landscape and patchwork fields, the granite hedges and strange rock formations, the old mine buildings beyond St Just, and always the backdrop of a jade sea that turns to deep purple.

In my mind run the words of that resounding poem written by John Heath-Stubbs:

> This is a hideous and wicked country,
> Sloping to hateful sunsets and the end of time,
> Hollow with mine shafts, naked with granite, fanatic
> With sorrow, Abortions of the past
> Hop through these bogs; black-faced, the villagers
> Remember burnings by the hewn stones.

With this background of horror-filled beauty, how can this part of the country be anything but a place of its own, with a particular character and atmosphere which has appealed to artists and writers from all over the globe? For this is the end of the country, sometimes feeling more like the end of the world. And, yet, as far as I am concerned, the most spellbinding drive you could wish to take lies on the winding road between St Just and St Ives. Every corner opens up new views of staggering dimensions. There is a flinty drama to the place which never fails to stir. It is a dangerous journey for it is all too easy to lift your eyes to the views instead of concentrating on the hair-pin bends.

Mine buildings at Botallack built into the cliff—the workings of this mine extended under the seabed to a depth of over a hundred fathoms in the nineteenth century and the miners worked with the sound of the breakers overhead.

It is typical of this part of Cornwall that many of the farms are small, some only a few acres, and yet families have managed to make a living from small pockets of land. One such character is Peter Thomas. To me he embodies much that is best in the Cornish people. He knows and respects his part of the country; he was born and brought up just outside St Just. He married his cousin Enid and together they have enjoyed their life which cannot always have been easy, but they obviously have a natural aptitude to

make the most of what they have. They never had the opportunity to leave West Cornwall and their son—who has—finds that he does not want to.

They know the moorland slopes and the rock formations; they know the coves and beaches; they know the history of the mines and can remember a time when many of their friends and neighbours were concerned with the mining industry.

Peter's father moved to the little hamlet of Truthwall in 1925 and bought forty acres of land which he handed over to Peter and his brother in 1945. Once the brothers ran a dairy herd but when so much modern machinery was needed to keep up to date, they sold their cows and started vegetable growing. Now they have delivery rounds selling their own carrots, broc-

The small patchwork fields of West Cornwall near Zennor ... a treeless landscape with granite hedges and strange granite formations ...

Peter and Enid Thomas: 'To me he embodies much that is best in the Cornish people.'

coli and potatoes. It's well to remember most people in Cornwall refer to cauliflowers as broccoli.

Peter's childhood and boyhood were spent in the area and he immersed himself in village life at a time when everyone knew everyone else and the highlights of the year revolved round cricket and football matches, singing in Methodist choirs and attending the village school. When Peter moved from Carnyforth school to Penzance it was quite a shock for him to suddenly find himself amongst so many children. There were extra pupils at that time who had been evacuated from Devonport High School during the war.

Now Peter has built his own house with his own hands on the hill just outside St Just with wonderful views stretching down to Truthwall, past the little fields and houses, to that great timeless seascape beyond. One February day when I visited Peter and Enid we could see the rocks of Land's End and then in the further distance the Isles of Scilly. In between these land masses lies the Lost Land of Lyonesse, that mythical underwater world that has so captured the imagination of many people from geologists to poets, novelists and artisans alike. Now there is a new fascination with that area for hundreds of dolphins have been discovered there and have turned it into a sort of Dolphin City.

Peter has filled his house with the books and records which ensure his leisure hours are spent in learned enjoyment. His favourite author is Neville Cardus who mixed his love of music and cricket in his books, the two subjects which have so captivated Peter all his life. Woe betide those who think this is a land of forgotten uneducated people. To listen to Peter talk about music is to listen to a real expert. He remembers well going to Plymouth as a lad of seventeen and hearing Benjamino Gigli sing. Gigli was fifty-nine years old then and Peter explains, 'His voice was as tremendous as ever.'

One fine bright afternoon, in clear winter light, I walked with Peter down past the village of Botallack to the famous mine buildings called Crowns. They are probably among the most picturesque of mine buildings, built as they are into the rocky cliff face with waves breaking relentlessly below. The workings of this mine extended under the seabed to a depth of over a hundred fathoms in the nineteenth century and the miners worked with the sound of the breakers overhead.

It was a dark and dismal world for the miners. From dawn to dusk they worked underground, only seeing the light of day on Sundays. No wonder that the Blind

Miner of Botallack became a king in that dark underworld. For when the other miners were in difficulties because their candles had gone out he could lead them wherever they wanted to go. His blindness turned into an advantage. As D.M. Thomas wrote in his poem *Botallack*,

He was blind,
In the country of the blind, that man was king.

Sundays were light days for the underground workers and most of them attended chapel meetings and sang the Wesley hymns that seemed to cheer them. There were some great preachers in those days and there are still many stories abounding of the more eccentric preacher John Willie Thomas. On the subject of the colour bar he was heard to exclaim: 'In the sight of Almighty God—and the Queen—all men are level.' Once Peter Thomas remembers him walking out in the middle of a service, leaving his congregation aghast. When he returned he explained that he had seen a friend riding past on his bicycle and he had gone out to ask him to come in and join them. He saw nothing at all strange in his actions.

There are so many memories for Peter Thomas to look back on. He climbed over those cliffs around Botallack all through his childhood and fished from the rocks with a long bamboo fishing rod. Yet when I asked him where he went to swim he looked at me aghast. He cannot swim, would not swim, and is always trying to persuade visitors not to swim. Like most Cornishmen he has a healthy respect for the sea and has seen the disasters it can cause.

In the old mine chimneys he and his boyhood friends once burned some dried gorse and watched the chimneys smoking against the summer sky. How innocent they thought their pleasure. But it was during the second world war and next day they heard that Lord Haw Haw had included in one of his treacherous broadcasts that the mines of the South West seemed to be working again and it was time they were paid a visit. A week later Peter watched as aeroplanes flew above the mines and there were bursts of machine gun fire and bombs were dropped. He was convinced that it was all on account of the childhood prank and was quite terrified at the consequences.

One of the nicest stories I have heard tell of the Cornish countryside came from Ray Bishop who took many of the photographs featured in this book. Some

Crowns at Botallack: Peter Thomas climbed these cliffs in his childhood and fished from the rocks.

Cornwall offers a grandstand view for spectacular sunsets.

Cyril Eddy and two of his horses. Not only does he still work horses on his land but he breeds pedigree shire horses.

time ago he was commissioned to photograph an old granite stone near St Buryan called the Blind Fiddler. He was told it was positioned in a field near the village and he set off, as he has so often done, to discover his subject. He wandered about in the district for some time before he spotted the large rather strangely-shaped piece of granite, but to his amazement there, ploughing in the same field, was a man and his two horses. For a minute he felt that he had gone back in time, that perhaps those Cornish piskies were playing one of their tricks on him.

But soon he was chatting to the ploughman and discovered he was Mr Cyril Eddy, famous in those parts for having worked horses on his land long after others had given up, and for breeding the pedigree shire horses which seem to be increasing in popularity once more. Not only that. He has entered almost every ploughing competition throughout the country and has won more prizes than he says he cares to remember.

When Ray Bishop showed me the original photographs and told me the story, we decided to make a repeat journey to Trenuggo Farm to speak to this remarkable gentleman. 'Come on Wednesday next,'

Cyril Eddy ploughing his field — the Blind Fiddler in the background.

Lanyon Quoit — a Megalithic chamber tomb.
Throughout the years the people of Cornwall have known how to use their granite.

Mr Eddy said, 'I'll be doing some harrowing with the horses that day.'

When we arrived at the farm he was just harnessing up the great gentle animals. Juliet and Princess Margaret were the names of the pair. 'But we call this one Lady as I never did like the name Margaret for a horse,' he told me. Princess Margaret was already named when Mr Eddy and his son Robert bought her. Now she is a central part of the family. She is twenty-four-years old, has had seventeen foals and has entered and won many ploughing competitions. Her quiet sensible nature helped to control the less steady Juliet who was partnering her that day and is one of her offspring.

Mr Eddy's love of horses started at a very early age. He was three years old when his father first bought him a pony. It was nearly a missed opportunity as his father offered only £1 for the pony and the seller demanded £2. But Cyril Eddy burst into tears. 'I can remember it as if it were yesterday,' he told me, 'watching that pony being led away down the lane and thinking I had lost it. But fortunately when I started crying father gave in and bought him.'

By the time he was nine years old he was ploughing himself, after watching his father carefully from the sidelines, and he's been doing it ever since.

In the 1950s he almost gave up using horses but his son Robert was the one to encourage him back to the activity. When Robert was a teenager Mr and Mrs Eddy took to going out on Saturday evenings leaving their eldest son to baby sit with the young children. One evening when they returned they found Robert had all the old horse harness out on the kitchen table and was cleaning it. This continued for some weeks until Robert had all the harness gleaming and back to its old condition. It was then that he asked his father if he could try working with horses. Soon the beautiful beasts were back in use on the farm and one thing led to another until not only were they working with the horses and entering competitions but they were also breeding them for other people.

'Two years ago we entered a competition at Exeter and I was proud that there were three generations of my family taking part and six of my pedigree shire horses being worked there. That ought to go down in the *Guinness Book of Records*,' said Mr Eddy with a slow smile.

As I stood talking to him while he harnessed up the horses, a terrible hail storm came and I stood close to the sturdy animals to protect myself from the cold

The cross at the entrance to Boskenna.

wind and harsh hail stones which rained down unmercifully. Mr Eddy continued with his work undeterred by the weather.

'You don't even have a coat on,' I said, worried about this elderly man and the bitter cold. He looked up with his smiling blue eyes. 'I never wear more than this,' he said pulling out his thick jersey. 'I've never liked wearing a coat, and this is only a shower, it'll soon pass.' The black clouds above us seemed too ominous for his prediction to be true, but he was right. As soon as he had finished harnessing the two great mares, talking to them all the while, the sky suddenly brightened and the sun shone on their glistening flanks. Up and down the field he walked, calling words of command which sounded more like a song than an order.

Later Mr Eddy told me that they now have modern tractors on his two hundred acres of small patchwork fields with their granite hedges in this wild and unique part of Cornwall. But he still loves to work with his horses. 'You are never lonely. You can spend all day ploughing and drilling and harrowing with horses and you are always with a living thing. Nowadays tractors are fitted with radios and earphones and other devices but it's not the same as having a horse to talk to. And you can never doze off for they need constant attention.'

He breaks in all his own horses and has only once had a horse he could not break of bad habits. 'He kicked and kicked whatever you did. I expect if I had had a bit more time I could have managed him.'

In the field beyond us I could see the big stone, the Blind Fiddler, and in the field where we stood was another ancient granite standing stone. As far as Mr Eddy is concerned their main attribute is that they serve as a good rubbing stone for his cattle. That way his hedges and walls stay in good condition for the cattle never rub against them.

It is appropriate in a part of Cornwall where time seems to have stood still, that a man like Mr Eddy is keeping alive a farming custom that suits the place. And with a son and grandson who are showing interest in working with horses it looks as if there will be shire horses to be seen in the fields around St Buryan for some time.

Left: Mr Eddy loves to work with his horses. 'You are never lonely,' he says. Right: A more modern farming scene.

Cornish Gardens

Cornwall's gardens are some of the most picturesque and unusual in the whole of Britain for they harbour rare plants that grow well in the damp, mild climate; plants that cannot always be grown elsewhere on this island. Added to the advantage of a temperate climate is the fact that many Cornish men and women over the years have become avid gardeners: among others the Williams family of Caerhays Castle, the Bolithos of Trengwainton, the Quaker Fox family who came from the Falmouth area of Cornwall and owned many

Left: Glendurgan on the Hel-
ford River.   Right: Tremeer at
St Tudy.

Two views of the gardens at Lanhydrock, the home of the Robartes family on the River Fowey near Bodmin.

houses in that part including Glendurgan with its beautiful grounds. With their knowledge and enthusiasm they have made their gardens into shrines for the connoisseurs of the plant world.

The National Trust are now the guardians for some of Cornwall's most famous gardens once founded by the landed gentry of the county. Trelissick near Truro; Lanhydrock on the banks of the River Fowey, and home of the famous Liberal family the Robartes; Glendurgan; Cotehele, once the shooting lodge of the Mount Edgcumbe family with its sloping gardens leading right down to the wide sweep of the Tamar river, are just some examples.

Magnolias, rhododendrons, camellias and azaleas were collected from far-flung countries and have now made their home in Cornish gardens. It is the beauty of such rare plants and their unusual settings in the grounds of some of Cornwall's most beautiful houses that bring people from all over the world to admire and enjoy. It is not only the gardening fanatics who enjoy all this horticultural beauty but anyone who appreciates the beauties of Nature.

Lanhydrock is now run by the National Trust, guardians of some of Cornwall's most famous gardens.

In the nineteenth century plant hunting expeditions were sent abroad, often financed by Cornish patrons who were garden owners. From the plants they brought back cuttings, and seedlings have been swapped and lent and given from one part of the county to another so that through the generosity of these original innovators, their findings have spread from one famous garden to the next. The late George Johnstone was a great garden lover and maker and it was at his house, Trewithen, just outside Probus, that he set to work to create one of the most beautiful gardens now existing in Cornwall.

It is probably most famous for its huge yellow rhododendron macabeanum which stands 20 feet tall and 30 feet across and when in full bloom has 500 trusses. It is a truly remarkable sight and was originally given to George Johnstone as a seedling by the late Sir Edward Bolitho of Trengwainton. There are also plants that have been propagated at the gardens like the ceanothus-arboreus 'Trewithen Blue' and a rhododendron named Trewithen Orange, a remarkable hybrid reared by George Johnstone.

Michael Taylor, head gardener at Trewithen, was awarded the Waley Medal in 1975 for the cultivation of rhododendrons.

When he inherited Trewithen in 1904 there was much to be done. His predecessors had landscaped it, that was the gardening art of the eighteenth century. They had also planted trees almost to a fault. In fact there was much clearing to be done before there was light and room enough to start laying out the rare plants that were to grow to such huge proportions over the next fifty years. In 1905 one hundred hybrids of rhododendron arboreum were planted. It was then that colour started to come into the garden for George Johnstone is reputed to have said that when he took over the gardens the only colour was lent by the washing when it was hung out to dry.

When trees were needed for shoring up the trenches in the first world war 300 beech trees were felled by government order and this laid open new vistas and spaces for wonderful plants of every colour and form and, in particular, the marvellous glade that stretches south from the front of the house.

A carpet of fallen petals at Trewithen, spring 1983.

I walked in the garden one sunny spring day with the head gardener Mr Michael Taylor who has been in charge of the gardens at Trewithen for the last seventeen years. In 1975 Mr Taylor was awarded the Waley Medal for the cultivation of rhododendrons, but when I asked him which was his favourite plant he found it hard to answer.

There is a time and a place for every plant in his life and his mind is always working ahead, replacing plants that have been lashed by storms, making sure that spaces are used well and with the most effect and propagating seedlings to be sold in the garden shop.

The height and width and colour of the many plants to be seen at Trewithen are something that leaves one full of admiration. There are special secluded corners, water gardens, a walled garden, wide open vistas leading away from the house and each part has a special atmosphere of its own created by what is growing there.

The beautiful wax-like buds of the magnolias were open when I was visiting and they seemed almost luminous in the strong spring sunshine like glowing

Trewithen is famous for its huge yellow rhododendron macabeanum which has as many as 500 trusses when in full bloom.

The beautiful wax-like buds of the magnolias were open when I was visiting Trewithen.

58

Huge tree ferns lend Trewithen a lush, almost tropical feel.

candles against the bright blue sky. The yellows and blues and deep reds and gentle pinks of the rhododendrons, the more delicate camellias with their heavy background of shiny leaves and the fan shaped and exotically coloured azaleas, many of which come from New Zealand and Australia, all lent their own type of beauty to this Cornish garden. And there are too the huge tree ferns, lush and almost tropical.

I could see and understand, as I talked to Michael Taylor, how a garden can become an obsession, for one can always be starting something new while retaining the best of the past. To wander amongst the plants that you have watched over so carefully, and to see them come into flower year after year lending a magic to each angle of the garden, must be truly satisfying and stimulating.

George Johnstone has certainly left a wonderful heritage to his successors at Trewithen. His grandson Michael Galsworthy with his wife and children live in the beautiful and classic house which lends such a fine backdrop to the garden. As I walked away that day through a carpet of camellia petals which were strewn on the ground forming a sort of bridal footpath I thought what more beautiful thing than a mature garden can a man leave to be enjoyed, not only by his heirs, but by all those who wish to venture here. It is fortunate for all garden lovers that these gardens are open to the public throughout the spring and summer in the afternoons.

Leaving the house, along the driveway through the parkland that surrounds it, I saw in the distance the white peaked mountains of the china-clay tips which lend a man-made beauty all of their own, and a typically Cornish backdrop.

'I saw in the distance the white peaks of the china-clay tips which lend a man-made beauty all of their own.'

Cornish Hedges

One of the more pleasing facets of the Cornish countryside is that many people are anxious to keep alive the old customs and crafts of this part of the Westcountry.

It is interesting, for instance, that many Cornish hedges are still being built in traditional style even alongside modern roads and town by-passes.

According to a handbook, *Dry Stone Walling*, published by the British Trust for Conservation Volunteers Ltd, 'all linear enclosing mounds which are not regular masonry are termed "hedges" in the mid and west Cornwall'.

One of the men responsible for several miles of stone hedging made in the last ten years in Cornwall is Roger Clemens. His love for working with stone started when he was on a farm up on Bodmin Moor in his early youth. Some mornings when there was not too much to be done he would be sent to help the older farm labourers repairing the hedges.

There he saw the men work almost instinctively with stone and earth and knew that they had learned this ancient craft from their fathers and predecessors before them. He was fascinated and intrigued by the craft which combined the skill of working with stone, setting it into a pattern that was both beautiful and practical, and the knowledge of how to make the structure strong and long lasting.

Most Cornish hedges are earth banks faced with stone and capped with turf. But in the far west dry stone hedges are common and down near Zennor there are some truly dramatic and unusual single rows of enormous granite boulders or 'grounders' which are sometimes as tall as seven feet and are relics of ancient enclosures, some maybe 2,000 years old.

Roger Clemens explained to me the elementary rules of building a hedge. The bottom must be as wide as the eventual height of the hedge and the inward curve or 'batter' strengthens the whole hedge. The topping design most often used in Cornwall is called 'herringbone', sometimes also referred to as 'Jack and Jill' or 'Darby and Joan'. Whatever its name it is the most beautiful design and uses up the smaller pieces of stone or chippings from the main part of the hedge. There are occasional hedges made entirely of herringbone design which are truly works of art.

The turf cap and earth filling given to the hedges are soon covered with all sorts of vegetation such as bracken and ferns, grasses and wild flowers of almost every variety from bluebells and campion to primroses and stitchwort and even wild orchids while the tougher gorse blazes its way down many a mile of Cornish hedge, both ancient and modern.

As someone remarked to me recently, 'You would have to be a modest man to be a Cornish stone hedger, for within a very small space of time no-one can see your work of art; it is so soon clothed in nature.'

'The difference between a Cornish hedge and a masonry wall is that one is a living thing and the other is not. It's as simple as that,' Roger Clemens told me as we talked one spring morning when he took a break

Of the Cornish Dame Barbara Hepworth said: 'They know how to put a stone into a wall instinctively; it fits just right and at the first attempt.'

'Since I spent the morning with Roger Clemens I have been fascinated by the many patterns and styles of hedging to be seen … a craft which combines the skill of working with stone and setting it into a pattern which is both beautiful and practical.'

'You would have to be a modest man to be a Cornish stone hedger, for in a short space of time no-one can see your work of art; it is soon clothed in nature… bracken and ferns, grasses and wild flowers of almost every variety from bluebells and campion to …

… primroses and stitchwort and even wild orchids while the tougher gorze blazes its way down many a mile of Cornish hedge …'

Hedgerows provide a habitat not only for flowers but also for many forms of wildlife. The weasel, above, a highly efficient predator, was trying to retrieve a freshly killed rabbit by the roadside. The grey squirrel, right, is appealing but a pest to foresters as he strips the bark from trees and also eats eggs and nestlings.

from his labour. He does some very fine masonry work of all descriptions but he remains proudest of all of his Cornish hedges. He has been responsible for the longest piece of stone hedging done recently in the county which is five miles long on the Marazion by-pass. He uses a slate type of stone in mid and north Cornwall and yellow granite from Castle-an-Dinas in

the west of the county. He likes to always choose his own stone from the quarry.

'It's no wonder people have a saying in Cornwall, "He eats like a hedger",' Roger Clemens told me. 'We have to work out in all weather and so we always have a good appetite. There is plenty of hard physical work when you're hedging but it is satisfying,' he added.

He has many young people applying for work with him and he says he knows within minutes whether they will make good hedgers. 'You can tell by the way they handle the stone whether they will have a feel for it,' he said. 'The strange thing is that good bricklayers don't often make good hedgers.' He has an excellent young man working with him now called Keith Gregory, who is proving to be a true craftsman, and it is comforting to know that the younger generation will keep the work going.

Some people object to the old hedging methods being used on the new roadsides saying there are less expensive ways of fencing off property and that this work is a waste of time and money. But Roger Clemens claims that they are worth every penny spent on them. They last for generations if well built, they give shelter to stock in the fields which ordinary fencing does not, and they are things of beauty as well.

Since I spent the morning with Roger Clemens talking about hedges in the Cornish countryside I have been fascinated by the many patterns and styles of hedging to be seen. I look out for them, often having to peer through all kinds of thick undergrowth to see what pattern or type of stone laying has been used.

It is good that Cornwall County Council still makes use of this craft along its highways and by-ways ensuring that the art will remain part of our heritage, for it is estimated that thousands of hedges are bulldozed away each year to make room for larger fields which are easier to manage.

The other day I noticed a farmer who lives nearby had rebuilt part of his hedging adjacent to a new gate. It gave me a great thrill to see that in amongst the stones he had made a gallant attempt to replant the primrose plants. It reminded me of Roger Clemens' remark about hedges being 'living things'.

Above: A curious view of Plymouth from a Cornish window in the grounds at Mount Edgcumbe.
Left: Three-Hole Cross near Wadebridge on the Camelford road.

*The Cornish have applied their skill with wall building in
many directions — here a tide mill in the Camel Estuary
near Padstow.*

Cecil Billing— Blacksmith

In the last century and the beginning of this the centre of farm and village life was the smithy. There the gifted blacksmith would mend ploughshares, make tools to be used on the land and shoe the horses that did the majority of the work. With skill they wrought wheels for carts and performed all sorts of tasks which kept life going on the farm and in the home. Without a blacksmith the country people could not have existed and these men were truly craftsmen, often learning their trade from their fathers before them.

One such blacksmith I have known for several years. Cecil Billing later turned his expertise into an art form and, having painted all his life, started to sculpt in iron. Now he is settling down to serious writing, hoping to preserve some of the old customs and sayings that were prevalent in his youth by stitching them into the story of his life.

Cecil was brought up at Dunstan's Farm, St Mellion, where his father was in charge of the horses. Now much of that land has been incorporated into the new golf course.

As a lad Cecil suffered much hardship when he contracted tuberculosis in his leg. He spent many months having treatment in hospital in Plymouth and was always a sickly child although he learned remarkably quickly how to get about with an iron paten on his shoe and with the help of crutches.

His first experience as a blacksmith was when he used to go to the smithy at Paynter's Cross at the gates of Pentillie Castle to have his built-up boot fixed. He

can remember the thrill of watching Mr Deacon, the blacksmith at that time, as he worked away with great ingenuity. From time to time Cecil was allowed to 'pull the cow horn on the end of a stick which worked the bellys to blow the fire.'

Years later he was to look back with admiration on that man's skill when he set to work himself as a blacksmith at Torpoint. He enjoyed designing new implements for farmers or finding special ways of fixing and improving ploughs that were brought to him in a damaged condition. He says that the second world war meant 'agriculture had to pull its socks up although people didn't like being dictated to by the government'; and many farmers were to learn a whole new concept of ploughing.

'Everything at the beginning was experimenting. There was a complete revolution in farming techniques at that time and the horse was slowly phased out as the Ferguson machinery came in.'

From 1939 to 1950 Cecil Billing worked with the firm of Watkins and Roseveare. He became intrigued with methods of welding and experimented with different metals. Then he went on a fact-finding tour of Britain, collecting ideas in all the major towns and still keeping up his drawing and painting. 'All engineering starts with drawing. Whether you work with wood or iron you have to be able to see what you are working towards,' he told me.

Now there is nothing that Cecil Billing will not contrive to make in metal. He loves the designing as much as the practical welding and turning. He once came to my house to design an iron basket for the fireplace. For a while he was the artist as he sat and sketched and the final product was so perfect; beautiful and yet practical and fitting for the room. The artist and the engineer had come together in a fine piece of work.

He once constructed a spiral staircase; he has forged wrought-iron gates; and he always enjoys making fire baskets and repairing old and antique ones with great care. The strangest thing he was ever asked to produce was a gate that would keep a tortoise in and he once designed a special ring for a pig's muzzle so that it would not dig up the ground.

In the garden of his home at Quethiock where he now lives he has a little studio and there he settles to his painting and his writing. His working shed is three or four times the size of his studio and full of Heath-Robinson machinery and hundreds of tools, everything from a pair of pliers to a wonderful contraption for pulling up brambles and dandelion roots.

It is marvellous to hear Cecil Billing talk about his

Cecil Billing (above left) in his workshop, which is full of Heath-Robinson machinery and tools.

childhood. It could have been an entirely miserable one for he suffered so much illness and his mother died when he was still very young and in and out of hospital himself. But, growing up on a farm with a large family, there were many pleasures to be found in life and none of them were missed by the lame child who showed so much guts, and when he simply could not keep up with his brothers and sisters he was happy to while away his time reading.

He talks of the work on the farm, of the only car in the vicinity being owned by the vet, about the Cherry Feasts given at Pentillie Castle for all the children of the neighbourhood, of the school teacher at St Mellion School and the chapel services at Polborder and Bealbury. Rules were rules then, family life was strict, what father said was sacrosanct, and everyone did their bit towards keeping the house going. But Christmas and holidays and festivities took on a special meaning and celebrations were far more deeply enjoyed.

Those were the days of hayricks and the first combine harvesters, of horses performing most of the heavy work on the farms, of reeds for 'datching' ricks after the harvest. A farmer's work was never done.

Cecil has written in his memoirs, 'Still all the hard work, the heat and the sweat was forgotten when the Missus and one of the maids with the "chullern" came out with the drinkings. A pure white cloth was spread in a shady place and cups laid for the men, a huge wicker basket was filled with bread and farm-made butter, tarts and saffron cake, enough for all including the children and the dog. Tea was poured from a copper kettle glinting in the sunlight from much polishing. After all had been satisfied pipes or Woodbines would be lit, the quality of the hay discussed, whether to start making out the rick before they got to "vorends" (fore ends) and the man on the sweep gave his opinion that there was enough hay in the "vorends" to make out the rick, and so all was settled.'

What a way to end the day.

Cecil Billing

Harvesting at Erth Barton near Saltash.

Mr and Mrs Jack Andrew

Often enough when passing a field of sheep one sees a black lamb amongst the flock. It is not an unusual sight. But in the spring of 1983 we found a farmer who had twenty-one black sheep, a rare sight in Cornwall.

John Tremaine Andrew has been working with sheep for the last seventy years. His unusual flock of black lambs came about when he borrowed a friend's black Welsh ram for his ewes, and so all his white ewes gave birth to black lambs that year, twenty-one black lambs from seventeen white ewes.

Mr Andrew—'I'm known as Jack by everyone around here'—is only working seven and a half acres now but he has been farming ever since he left school at the age of fourteen and went home to Trevethan Farm, near Padstow, where his father and his grandfather had farmed before him. He had been longing to leave school and get down to 'man's work'. But now he says he regrets leaving so soon as he has often found difficulty with jobs which involved much reading and writing.

Jack Andrew ploughed and worked with horses and never got used to using a tractor. 'It was all right until things went wrong. I never was good with machinery. I knew what I was doing with a horse, though.'

Jack was happily married and worked away at his farm until his wife died in 1961, but luckily for him he met the perfect second wife whom he married in 1966. She presented him with three step children. 'They've all been very good to me and made up for the fact that I never had any children.'

His second wife, Joyce, had also farmed all her life and they continued to work on her farm at St Erny until they decided to move to Bodmin Moor. Jack was seventy two years old when they moved to Menabroom Farm. 'A lot of people thought it was a mad thing to do at my age.' But they were never so happy. 'I'm easy to transplant and have never minded moving,' Jack says. Those years on the moor were the most successful of all his years farming. 'But when we left Menabroom I really minded leaving.' Like so many other people who farm on the moor, Jack and his wife lost their hearts to the place and still talk about it with a sincere warmth.

'My wife and I and my stepson ran that place on our own and we managed very well. When the time came to bring the corn in we three would work together and all went smoothly until my wife started taking more notice of the badger tracks than she did of the filling sacks; then everything went for six.' He laughs at the memory.

Both Jack and Joyce loved riding and rode to hounds on their two old cobs and they also used them for rounding up the cattle on their moorland farm. They have a goat who has been with them several years and who once went under the name of Gorgeous. 'But when he jumped through the roof of my landrover and cost me £20 we changed his name to Ghastly,' Jack told me, sharing an old joke.

Jack and Joyce moved down from Bodmin Moor a few years ago to their little bungalow at St Merryn

Mr and Mrs Jack Andrew with their old horse, Rennie, who served them well on Bodmin Moor and the Ghastly Goat.

Jack Andrew's unusual flock of black lambs — in 1983 he had 21 black lambs from 17 white ewes — a rare sight in Cornwall.

where they are very happy with their seven acres of land, their seventeen ewes, their twenty-one lambs, their two old horses—'They've served me well so I'll let them live out their days here until they have to suffer, then I'll see they don't,' Jack told me—the Ghastly goat, two dogs and a cat.

The view from the house looks out across fields, over one of the most beautifully designed stone Cornish hedges I have ever seen, down to the sea and the Quies rocks. These rocks, which are called the Cow and Calves by the local people, are the Andrews' favourite weather forecasters. When the sea is high

around them and you can see the waves breaking white against them then rain is sure to come. When it is calm like it was the day I was there then rain will not come for a while. It's never been proved wrong so far and that day although rain had been predicted on the official weather forecast it was a beautifully sunny day, just as the rocks said it would be.

People like John Tremaine Andrew, otherwise known as Jack, have seen many changing fortunes in their lives. 'When I first married we used to take the horse and cart down to the beach of an evening and collect sand for the builders. We were paid 1s. 6d. a

Jack Andrew at Trevethan Farm in the 1930s with the Horn Speed Binder. It was after the second world war that combine harvesters first came to Cornwall.

load. I can remember it well, and we were most grateful for that at the time,' Jack told me.

He professes to be a mean man, never spending money when it is not absolutely necessary, but the more he told me about his life, about how a farmer, in his youth, never ever borrowed money, never ever dared to have an overdraft, the more I realised how clever he had been to build up a little fortune over the years which he seems to have given away to his family with a rashness not usually seen in a mean man.

He regrets nothing except leaving school so early, is amazed at his own good fortune and says though he worked hard he never expected to do as well as he did.

His family were involved in local politics for over ninety years in the district and Jack played his part after his father and alongside his brother. He is proud of what he has done, has obviously enjoyed his life enormously and with his charming manners and gentle, but spritely and mischievous ways he is part of a generation now dying out. There will never be men in the new generation who will see such changes, who will gain and give away so much, who will work so hard and yet at the age of 84 still show signs of doing quite a lot in the future.

Steam Engines

Just as the cart and horse and carriage have given way to the car so the engines of farming have greatly changed in the last forty years. Most of the machinery on farms used to be driven by steam and there are a group of people who are still thrilled and deeply interested in these picturesque machines.

Just beyond Little Petherick on the north coast is a farm called Trevillador owned by the Prideaux-Brune family, but run by tenant farmer, Mr Hingston Wood, and two of his sons. The family are all deeply involved with the land and take great interest in the eighty acres.

Richard, Hingston Wood's son, grew up with a passion for steam engines. It was on Christmas Eve 1956 that he saw a magnificent steam engine driving through the lanes from Wadebridge when it had just arrived in Cornwall. He thought then, although he was only a boy, what a wonderful thing it would be to own such a bit of machinery. Ten years ago he became the proud owner of this machine called Challenger and over the years he says it has become part of him. He talks of the machine as if he were talking about a person and says one should always refer to steam engines in the female gender. 'She is a real beauty,' he says stroking her gleaming brass and maroon sides.

Originally Challenger was built as a fairground machine but she was also used for bio-scopes, the first form of film shows. Then she was hauled around the fairgrounds generating electricity for the horse merry-go-rounds. She was made by the firm of Burrell's who vied with Fowler's to be the most famous steam engine manufacturers.

Challenger was a Showman's Road Locomotive and is a truly beautiful object. I went to see her in the great barn at the farm where other steam engines are also stored. Some belong to friends of Richard Wood, since steam engine fanatics are inclined to flock together.

One machine in this barn was called The Farmer's Friend and she once performed a lot of the work on the farm such as sawing, thrashing and stone crushing. Another old machine owned by Mr Jeff Westlake was used for cable ploughing and cultivating.

Steam died out just after the war when the combustion engine came into use. Steam was considered less practical because a steam engine had to be lit up at least an hour and a half before she was ready to work.

But Richard Wood has re-modelled an old threshing machine which they still use on the farm. It is particularly good at combing the sheaves of corn and preparing the reed ready for house thatching. Last March they worked seventeen acres with this marvellous old machine and the Woods have long been known as providers of excellent quality reeds for thatching. In fact thatchers throughout the country, many from Dorset and Hampshire and other counties, have bought the Hingston Wood reed. This all started only six years ago when Richard persuaded his father that there was enough demand to make it worthwhile.

Last year they travelled some seventeen miles to

Richard Wood is the proud owner of Challenger, a steam engine, built originally as a fairground machine.

Trebarwith with the machine and Richard Wood says it was hard work. They left his farm at 7.15 in the morning and did not arrive at the Trebarwith farm until 1.30 in the afternoon. Then they set to work and came home the next day.

It is wonderful to see how much pleasure these old machines still give. To work with them, Richard told me, was so different to working with modern machines. He admires every bit of craftmanship and sees them as a work of art as well as brilliant pieces of engineering. His pleasure comes from watching all the different parts of the engine in action and he says they are warm, almost living things as compared to modern machinery.

By the time I had spent a morning with Richard Wood climbing up on his machines and listening to him expound their merits I was lost in wonder and in love with them too.

Mr Hingston Wood, the father of four sons, William, Richard, James and Stephen, is a famous farmer in that part of Cornwall. He was a genius at ploughing with horses and won numerous prizes at St Mawgan when the present airfield was once competition plots for many of the ploughing competitions.

He is rightly proud of his sons and takes a keen interest in Richard's steam engines. On the day I visited the farm James's twins were referred to on several occasions. I thought them to be James's children but later discovered they were twin heifers, a rarity on this farm. It is only the third time that twin heifers have lived. Often twin calves are born on the farm but they are a bull and a heifer which makes it impossible to breed from the heifer as there is a hormone imbalance.

The Author examines one of Richard Wood's machines.

We went out to the shed to view the week old twins and could see they were James's pride and joy. He told me that once they had a calf born several weeks early and she was the smallest calf he had ever seen. The vet came and said he had no hope for it; it would surely die within a few hours. But this was a challenge to James who borrowed some babies' bottles from his sister-in-law and fed the calf every three hours. It lived and the vet pronounced it 'a real miracle'.

Farmers have to learn to harden their hearts if they are to do their jobs well and make a living but it is good to know that they can also feel deeply for their animals and be truly fond of them. There are nearly a hundred cows on the Wood's farm and James says he knows every one by name. While we were there he named the twin heifers Judy and Jenny.

In the big farm kitchen with benches and a large table we sat down to 'crib' and watched Richard eat huge slabs of fresh bread and treacle, which he says is his own form of engine oil. These men work hard outdoor lives starting very early and in the longer evenings not finishing till eight. They need their nourishment and their enjoyment and it is a strangely warming experience to sit amongst such a family, all working towards a common aim, all interested in each other's activities. The youngest son Stephen is a potter of great expertise. Richard took several things from his mother's china cupboard to show us what his brother had produced and we drank from elegant mugs made by Stephen. They obviously feel him to be a true artist and are sad that for the time being he has given up this occupation.

The Woods family now consider themselves Cornish as their father came to live here in 1945. Once again, I saw the pride of the father who is passing on his expertise and the profits of his hard labour to sons who have joined him in his work. Family units may have their difficulties but when they work, as they still seem to do in the countryside of Cornwall, there is a strength of bond and comradeship that is most moving.

As I left I admired some of the huge horseshoes on the wall outside the farmhouse which came from the hooves of horses Mr Hingston Wood once used for ploughing. He presented me with one saying he hoped it would bring me good luck and meanwhile James had cut some broccoli from their field for us to take away. Their hospitality and their enjoyment in life was obvious and left me feeling happy for the rest of the day.

James Wood with his twin heifers — a rarity on this farm.

Duchy Oyster Farms

In Cornwall you cannot divorce the countryside from the rivers and the sea—all three are related, moulding the very character of the county and, to a remarkable degree, its people. The rivers are not only set in some of the most beautiful, lush countryside, but they also contribute to Cornwall's employment and wealth.

Licensed fishermen still perform the ancient art of netting salmon and to watch them in the evening light on the River Tamar as the tide is turning below Cotehele quay or from Halton Quay a mile below the house where I live is to watch an ancient rite performed with a definite rhythm and strength.

It is hard work, of course, and only a strong man can let the nets out and then draw them in with proficien-cy and speed without letting the salmon escape. I have watched them for hours and heard the sworn irritation of the fishermen as some salmon jump high enough to escape the encircling net.

At Port Navas on an inlet of the beautiful Helford River another ancient rite is performed which has gone on since Roman times. The oyster farms there belong to the Duchy of Cornwall, are leased by MacFisheries and run by Mr Len Hodges. Len Hodges has been associated with oyster farming in this area since he was a boy. His father was an oyster fisherman and ran the same farm and his son is promising to run it when he retires in a few years' time.

Over a million oysters are sent out from Port Navas each year and most of them go to the plush restaurants and hotels of London where those who can afford to pay for them will enjoy this expensive fish. The oysters are sold from the farms for just over £5 for ten, but by the time they get to the dinner table they will cost twice this amount.

Oyster farming has become more skilled over the years. No longer do the boats just go out to dredge them off the beds of the Helford River. Now the fishermen must think of conserving their fish and seed and other fish are brought from all over the world to lie and fatten on the river's bed.

They take at least four years before they are fat enough to be eaten and many of the oysters which are brought off the bed of the river are returned if they are not considered big enough for the market.

Durgan on the Helford River.

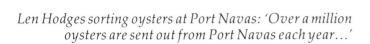

Len Hodges sorting oysters at Port Navas: 'Over a million oysters are sent out from Port Navas each year...'

In the little factory at Port Navas the fish are graded in a machine which drops them off into baskets according to their size and weight. Then they are packed in little round wicker baskets with a padding of seaweed. The end product is so attractive that one feels this is more a work of art than a farming or factory process.

Lately there has been a killer disease, Bonamia, which has probably come from abroad and has destroyed thousands of oysters in the area. It has meant that movement of young oysters has been curtailed for the time being.

Len Hodges enjoys his work to the full and told me that his father enjoyed his work exactly as he does. Len's son will be the fifth generation of his family to work in oyster farming. It is a proud boast of Len's that the tradition is carrying on.

Above the little cove of Port Navas Len Hodges lives in a house with a view, typical of Cornwall's river creeks, looking out over the lawn across the little bay and with a view of the oyster farm buildings in the distance. He reckons he can keep an eye on the place at all times and it is obvious that his life has been devoted to running the farm efficiently and keeping up the very high standards.

When Prince Charles, the Duke of Cornwall, and his new wife visited the county in 1983 they were given a meal entirely made up of food grown on Duchy land and one of the courses was oysters cooked in a delicate sauce of cream, lemon juice and cheese.

The farm employs ten people and has four boats, two working from Port Navas, one from Falmouth and one from Percueil. Every day dredging takes place. Immediately after the war oysters were so popular in England that they were all sold in this country.

Recently the sales to Belgium have gone up and Mr Hodges is exploring the likelihood of selling to Holland as well. Today, about 35 to 40 per cent of their oysters are exported.

'I've enjoyed every minute of my life,' says Len Hodges. His father retired when he was over seventy, and then only because of illness. Len Hodges does not think he will leave it as late as that as he has lots of other interests. But he will miss the work and will almost certainly stay in the village of Port Navas where he owns a beautiful house down near the quay.

Of course things have changed in Port Navas like everywhere else. Many of the houses are now second holiday homes for people who live outside the area and some flamboyantly designed modern houses have been built on the sloping land by the river. But there is an atmosphere there that lingers on. Len Hodges can well remember coming home from chapel on a Sunday and hearing strong language from the ship's chandler, where the sailors played their games of cards. At that time most trading was done by sea and sailing boats came up the river to unload. It was a seagoing and fishing community. Sounds, smells and sights have changed greatly in Len Hodges' lifetime. Will his son see as much change during his?

One regret for Mr Hodges is that the Royal family have not shown a great liking for oysters. He has never sent a consignment to Buckingham Palace although the late Duke of Windsor, when Prince of Wales, was very fond of them.

The real connoisseurs of oysters like them best straight from the shell and visitors sometimes come to Port Navas to sit on the quay and eat their oysters with a bottle of wine and some brown bread and gaze out over the river.

The Royal Cornwall Show: '…easily the most important annual event in the Cornish farmer's calendar.'

Royal Cornwall Show

Easily the most important annual event in the Cornish farmer's calendar is the Royal Cornwall Show. One of the oldest agricultural shows in the country, its origins date back as far as the eighteenth century. The event has become a way of life in Cornwall.

Schools are almost empty on these occasions as it is a family outing and since time immemorial children have gone along with their parents whatever stage they may have reached at school. Some headmasters, who have come from outside the county to work in schools in Cornwall, have been shocked and, in some cases, full of disapproval to find their classrooms empty for at least one of the days in June when the Royal Cornwall Show is in full swing. But most of them have had to come to expect and accept this mass exodus towards the showground, now on a permanent site just outside Wadebridge where the Royal Cornwall Agricultural Association owns 165 acres of land.

I went to visit Mr Albert Riddle who has become part of the Royal Cornwall since he has been responsible for running the show for more than a quarter of a century. Here is a man who truly loves his job. 'I don't expect there are many men who can say they love every single moment of their work,' he told me as he sat behind his desk in the smart office building on the show ground answering last minute telephone queries about the Show. It was in March that I visited him and bookings for space and entries had already long been made but there are always late enquiries.

The Cornwall Agricultural Society was started with first official membership in 1792. At that time it was a travelling show moving from one place to another each year. Mr Riddle showed me some of the first documents they have of a show held in 1803 at Bodmin with lists of the prizes. Of course the ploughing competitions at that time were performed by oxen and I was surprised how big the prize money was, the highest being for the sum of ten guineas. A lot of money for those days.

The Royal Cornwall Show is now considered to be one of the top eight agricultural shows in the United Kingdom. It all started on a much smaller scale when in 1803 the Society had a total of 194 subscribers who were mainly members of the 'Gentry' and wealthy farmers with a few businessmen. It is interesting to note the continuity amongst those involved with the Society over the years. Those families taking part in the 1803 Show who are still involved today include the Boscawens (the present Lord Falmouth is Chairman of the Association), the Bolithos (Mrs Simon Bolitho was the 1980/81 President), the St Aubyns, the Molesworths (Sir John Molesworth St Aubyn is a past Chairman of the Association), the Carews and the Vyvyans.

The granting of the Royal Charter came in 1827 and marked the turning point from a county show into a highly-regarded agricultural exhibition with people travelling from all over the country to take part.

In 1858 the Association decided to hold the Show in

Albert Riddle — 'Mr Royal Cornwall'.

At the Royal Cornwall Show in 1875 at Truro. The President, Mr Edward Archer in the grey top hat and side whiskers is standing beside his wife seated in the white dress.

alternate years in the east and west of the county: Camborne one year Launceston the following.

It was in 1960 that the Show first was held on the permanent site near Wadebridge. Until 1976 this wonderful site which has proved so successful in every way was leased from the Duchy of Cornwall. In 1976 the Duchy generously offered the Association the chance to purchase the show site, 76 acres of land, at the low cost of £15,000. The transfer was completed in 1977.

Since then an old farmyard and a further three acres have been purchased which has allowed for an extension to the showground and after much work on the land there are sites for the Steam Fair, 62 trade stands and a leisure and picnic area. So the place grew and grew. Now there is a huge cattle barn, built at the cost of £46,000 and many roads and parkways have been constructed.

The running of the Show has become big business and it is important to make the place and buildings pay for themselves between Shows. So there is now a 300 unit caravan and camping site, and the ground is hired out for all sorts of gatherings, parties and weddings. Any function from 60 to 4,000 people can now be accommodated in one or other of the buildings. All profits are ploughed back into the showground to improve facilities for exhibitors and public alike.

The turnover of the Royal Cornwall Agricultural Association is now on the way to being a quarter of a million, so Albert Riddle, by force of circumstance, has had to become a businessman as well as an agricultural expert.

His love of the job and the people he has worked with through the years is obvious and he says the responsibility lies heavily on his shoulders to continue to make it a great success each year. But his obvious enthusiasm is contagious and both his wife and his son help him in the office so that it has become

Prince Charles, Duke of Cornwall, presents the prizes in 1977.

Conversation Piece at the Royal Cornwall Show

an all-consuming family affair. Albert Riddle hopes that his son, Chris, will one day take over his job.

Mr Riddle told me that the greatest change in his time took place when the travelling Show came to a permanent site. But he says, 'I am a traditionalist and have tried my best to keep it a traditional agricultural show and I jealously guard that.'

He has worked happily with members of the Council, Presidents, exhibitors and tradespeople alike and it is obvious that one of the reasons for his success is that he likes people and understands the essence of his home county of Cornwall. He told me: 'You can lead a Cornishman with a piece of cotton but you can never drive him anywhere.' It summed up for me so much about the Cornish character and it was fine to hear a man who is proud to be Cornish putting it into words; for it was not only an understanding of his fellow countrymen he offered but an understanding of himself as well.

Forceful, decisive and so clearly a man who has spent his life happily he is well-known to almost all country people in Cornwall and most people consider

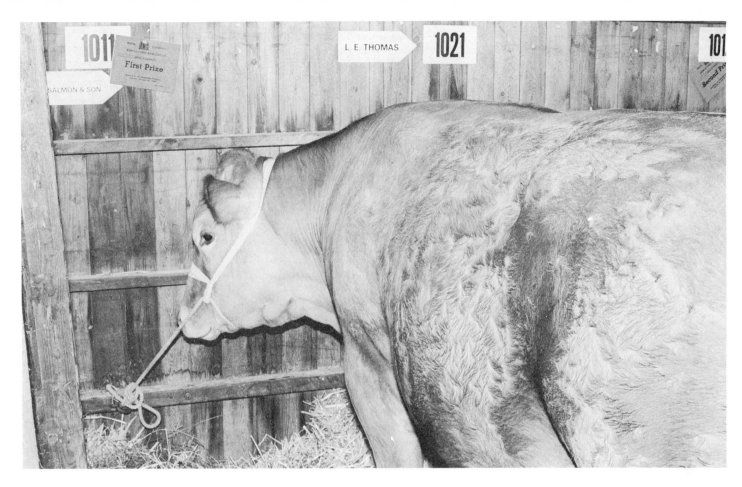

A Prizewinner at the Show

him Mr Royal Cornwall Show. He has had to deal with many difficulties and dramas over the years. On one occasion when the Show was being held at Truro there was a terrible gale the night before and every building and tent was brought to the ground. No-one thought the Show would go on—but it did. In 1957, when Mr Riddle first took over, the Suez Canal crisis caused the loss of many of the trade stands which nearly wrecked the Show.

It was during Mr Riddle's time that showjumping became a major part of the Show attracting many of the top showjumpers in the country. The flower tent at the Royal Cornwall is also one of its main features and draws people from miles around; over the years this magnificent display of flowers and their arrangements has grown and constantly demands more space. So with the steam fair, the local crafts tent, the wonderful flowers and of course the excellent entries of horses, cattle, sheep and pigs, dogs, poultry, cage birds, pigeons, bees and honey there is enough to interest and educate the 90,000 people who will visit the Royal Cornwall Show in June in every year.

Cider Making

In the season of 'mellow fruitfulness' when the climate of Cornwall can be at its mildest, gentlest and most appealing, I went to take part in a day's cider making at Westcott Farm just outside Callington.

A group of keen revivalists of old customs had come together to make cider in the traditional way, using a well preserved cider press on the farm belonging to the Hambly family. I have often gone to see old cider presses, some in better condition than others but had never seen one in use before.

In 1980 I went to talk to Mr J.E. Pearce who was a famous cider-maker from St Veep. There he showed me his old cider press and explained how it was still used in the traditional manner.

Later he took me to the room where his cider was stored in old wooden barrels and we sat on a bench in the shed and tasted some of his most delicious vintage cider. He told me at the time that the taste of cider depended on many things. The type of apple used, the type of barrel it was stored in and what had been kept in the barrel before, and also how long the cider was left to mature. The best barrels, Mr Pearce told me, were old port and rum barrels, but he could no longer obtain the rum barrels that he had once used.

He recited to me the names of the apples that he had used over the many years that he had been making cider. Bulmers Norman, Yarlington Mill, Crimson King, Morgan Sweet, Ellis's Bitter, Sweet Coppin— wonderful names made even richer sounding in his strong Cornish accent.

I learned from Mr Pearce that there is a pride in producing real cider and I could see that with him it had become a way of life. Over the years he must have

The apple crusher — the stone is pulled round by the horse.

made thousands of gallons. Sadly, not long after I visited him, he died and I was unable to ever see him actually in the process of making cider. So it was with great excitement that I joined the group at Westcott Farm.

On arrival at the old cider press I immediately became aware that this was not only a job of work but a kind of celebration. It was during a weekend and all those involved had come. Some had brought sacks full of apples; one woman had brought her horse who was of a quiet nature and suitable for pulling the great granite crushing stone. Children were there and also those who knew how to weave the cheese of straw between each layer of apples.

The smell in that little stone shed was sweet and strong: of pressed apples and a working horse and many people hard at work. It is a spectacle to be enjoyed but those who are just there to watch are likely to get in the way for there is plenty of action and little space.

Apples have to be put into the round stone trough and then the horse is led around attached to the great grinding stone. The crushed apples are transferred to the cheese and the special straw woven around each layer until enough layers have been built to reach the top of the press.

When the press is brought down to squeeze the juice of the apples through the straw and into the buckets below, it must be done gently. The greatest danger is that the cheese will become lopsided and the whole thing collapse, and all the hard work ruined.

Watching the expertise and the work involved I was reminded yet again how farming and agricultural jobs once involved many people so that a whole family felt part of the work. In fact it was often impossible for a farmer or agricultural labourer to operate properly without the help of his wife and children.

The pulp is laid between layers of straw to make a 'cheese' for pressing to extract the juice.

95

Churches and Chapels

Just as the relics of old mining buildings are part of the Cornish countryside so are the chapels and churches an integral part of its landscape and its heritage. Without them the county would be lacking in much of its character.

Often when driving through the lanes a church tower will peep over the thickly-growing hedgerows and if you stop and enter you will find all sorts of treasures that are part of the history of that area.

Some churches have early stained glass often de-picting stories of the Cornish Saints. There are bench ends with interesting carving recording the myths and legends which belong to the country of Cornwall.

Often these churches nestle in beautiful situations like the church at St Just in Roseland, the garden of Cornwall. As the Poet Laureate wrote: 'This is to many people the most beautiful churchyard on earth, especially to those who think Roseland means land of roses, not of heath, which is the Cornish meaning of the word *Rhos.*'

The charm of this churchyard is that it lies in a hollow thickly clothed in flowering shrubs and trees, so that when you enter the lychgate the top of the tower seems to be at eye level. This spot feels hallowed and protected from the outside world and is full of a rambling, wild, natural beauty with river views beyond.

Another unusually sited church of Cornwall is at Blisland. This building is situated alongside the only village green in Cornwall. The green recently lost much of its glory when the elms were attacked by disease and many died and had to be cut down. But work has been done on replacing them, and many new trees have been planted. The fifteenth-century

Left: New trees planted on the village green at Blisland to replace the dead elms.   Right: Altarnun Church, known as the Cathedral of the Moor.

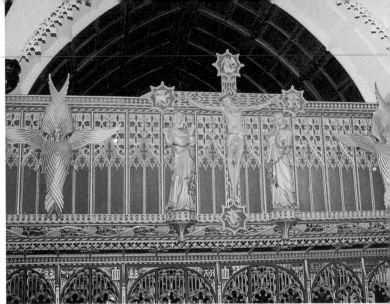

The screen at the Church of St Petroc Minor at Little Petherick — a beautiful addition this century.

'Lanteglos by Camelford has a fine, large church in a wooded valley ...'

church of St Protus and St Hyacinth is as beautiful inside as out with its barrel roof and granite pillars.

Lanteglos by Camelford has a fine, large church in a wooded valley with some remarkable stone crosses in the picturesque churchyard. I like the strength of the fifteenth-century tower.

I once stopped when driving from Wadebridge to Padstow to look inside the church of Little Petherick, St Petroc Minor. I was well rewarded, for this church, once again snuggled into a hollow above a tributary of the River Camel, is a surprise; it is so rich and ornate but in fine taste. From 1898 Sir Ninian Comper was employed by the patron, Sir Athelstan Riley, to embellish the church.

I think the delicately painted screen shown in the photograph is one of the most beautiful additions made this century to any of Cornwall's more ancient churches. It is typical of the surprises to be found if one cares to stop when out on a country drive and venture into the interior of one of many churches to be passed on all of Cornwall's major and minor roads.

Cornwall's Methodist chapels are stark and simple compared to her churches, but they remain a major part of the countryside and lend a special essence to the character of Cornwall.

Many of the chapels were built by the miners and

St Enodoc Church: A unique church, placed as it is in the centre of a golf course on the North coast of Cornwall near Rock, an area inevitably connected with the Poet Laureate, Sir John Betjeman. It was to this part of Cornwall he first came as a child and he was to write about it with loving nostalgia in his poems. One poem is centred on this church — 'Sunday afternoon Service in St Enodoc Church, Cornwall'.

Left: *A wedding in traditional style at
St Breock Church, near Wadebridge.
Right:*   *Ludgvan Church — the first
tower ever shaped by Cornish masons.*

The thatched chapel of Roseworthy as it was a few years ago.

fishermen and farmers in their meagre spare time and in a sense they were building a roof over their spiritual lives. They came to chapel to worship and to sing out the glad tidings of the Wesleyan hymns which resounded throughout the valleys and the high roads and lanes of the countryside. The division between chapel and church folk is still felt most strongly in Cornwall.

John and Charles Wesley encouraged their followers to build their own places of worship. Soon after came the shining example of Billy Bray, a hard working miner who was converted to Methodism and then walked miles preaching the gospel and helping to build at least three chapels in Cornwall.

Born and brought up in the parish of Kea in the

mining district of Gwennap, Billy Bray died in 1868. Sadly most of the chapels he built have become derelict but Baldhu Chapel still remains standing. There is a monument to Billy Bray in the churchyard of Baldhu.

The two chapels in the photographs depict very different styles. The thatched chapel of Roseworthy is now in private ownership and in a sad state of disrepair. The other more typical chapel of Cornwall is at Carharrack and built in memory of Billy Bray, as the tablet outside reads.

These are only a few of the churches and chapels that people our Cornish countryside, but no exploration of Cornwall is complete without some experience of them. They are part of the landscape and, more important, they have helped to shape the personalities of Cornish people. When we visit a chapel or church we're experiencing Cornish history.

A remarkable man, associated with both the Church and the land, who has helped in the making of Cornish history over the last sixty years is Canon Martin Andrews. He was Rector of Stoke Climsland Church from 1922–1968, befriended by the then

Carharrack Chapel, built in memory of Billy Bray, and the memorial to Billy Bray in the churchyard at Baldhu.

Prince of Wales, who became Edward VIII, and one of the most popular men in the area.

He is probably best known in Cornwall for his endeavours to help with the unemployment problem of the 1930s. With the encouragement of the Prince of Wales he developed a thriving market-garden business growing flowers and vegetables; from early beginnings when one man was employed he eventually was able to offer work to over fifty people. It was a major contribution to the region and one which people will never forget.

He became extremely interested and knowledgeable about flower and vegetable growing himself and, now that he has retired and lives in a house by the sea at Downderry, he continues to produce the most succulent tomatoes and hundreds of varieties of geraniums, all grown from seed. This gardening would be remarkable in any retired man, but the Canon is ninety-six-years young and so proud of his years that he often adds another to impress us even further.

No book about the countryside of Cornwall would be complete without the inclusion of the Canon. His particular form of joyful worship and preaching, his close involvement with the farming and gardening people of his parish over the years and his great compassion will long be remembered throughout Cornwall. Though not a Cornishman originally he has given so much of himself to the Cornish people that they have claimed him as one of their own.

St Piran's Cross

Canon Martin Andrews, Rector of Stoke Climsland Church from 1922–68, is best known for his endeavours to help the unemployed in the 1930s. Now 96 he still grows the most succulent tomatoes.

105

These five bridges probably span at least five centuries, from the early stone clapper bridges to the bridges across the Tamar: the famous Brunel railway bridge opened by Prince Albert in 1859 and the most modern of them all, the road bridge opened by the Queen Mother in 1962. These two bridges which span the last reaches of the Tamar by Saltash are where most people first glimpse Cornwall as they cross the boundary from Devon.

Below: Gam Bridge across the River Camel.
Right: Helland Bridge — note the different shape of the arches.

Brunel's railway bridge and the modern road bridge across the River Tamar.

A wooden bridge on the coastal footpath in Rocky Valley on the North Cornish coast.

Left: The Dipper is commonly found by Cornwall's fast-flowing moorland streams. He even walks underwater to feed.

Below: The dovecote at Cotehele House on the banks of the Tamar near Calstock. Cotehele dates back to the Middle Ages and is run by the National Trust.

The Tamar Valley

Many parts of the Tamar Valley are, happily, still largely undiscovered by visitors to the county. Along the last bends of the River Tamar there are still quiet, secret corners where life goes on much as it has done for two or three generations. There have been great changes too, for here, in the last century and the early part of this, vast amounts of the world's tin, copper, silver and arsenic were mined.

Now the old mine buildings stand derelict as reminders of that time when the valley was a centre of industry and when the river was a constant turmoil with barges and other vessels carrying lime, coal, wood and all the goods for the mining industry.

But alongside this industry ran the market gardens, some of them still in existence. The forty-seven different kinds of cherries once grown here are no

longer picked for commercial use, though their blossom still brightens the valley in the spring months. But the strip cultivation of flowers and vegetables and fruit is still practised to a certain extent and it is the patterns traced by these strips across the steep slopes that lend the Tamar Valley much of its character and beauty.

One flower-grower I spoke to is Nigel Hunn of St Dominic. He has been working with bulbs ever since he left school and his father and 'granfer' were also market gardeners before him. He has nearly forty acres of flowers and strawberries in the Tamar Valley and two nurseries with glass-houses where he produces chrysanthemums, irises and tulips. He also grows vegetables.

He sells his market produce in Dartmouth and Torbay and the rest goes to Hull and Birmingham. He employs five full-time staff and several casual workers, with the women still doing much of the bunching although they now also use a machine which Mr Hunn bought in Holland three years ago. 'It works a bit like a baler for hay,' he told me.

The year for Nigel Hunn and his fellow flower growers is 'governed by the weather', but he says Christmas time is the only fairly quiet period of the year. Usually picking of the bulbs begins in the first week of February and work starts at seven in the morning and goes on until about half past four. When I asked whether it was not back-breaking working on the steep slopes I was told that in fact it sometimes made it easier. He grows about twenty different types of daffodils, Dutch Master, Red Devon, Golden Ducket, Pheasant's Eye, White Lion being just some of their names. Inside the glass-houses over a quarter million irises are grown each year.

When the flower picking is over in April then the strawberry time starts and this lasts a couple of months. Nigel Hunn still enjoys getting up at six in the morning and joining the men who work for him as they pick the succulent fruit. He has an acre of cloches for his strawberries and supplies fifteen shops in Torbay, Tavistock and Holsworthy. He says that selling remains the hardest job of all and it is something he always does himself since personal contact still counts for a lot.

At the end of May when the 7,000 strawberry

Daffodils, once a prolific crop in the Tamar Valley, are still grown commercially.

Countryside and river in the Tamar Valley. Along the last bends of the river there are still quiet, secret corners where life goes on much as it has done for two or three generations.

cloches have all been stacked away Nigel makes a trip to Kent to buy new plants and bulbs. Every two or three years thirty tons of bulbs have to be lifted and sterilised at Fred Rogers' centre in St Dominic.

Meanwhile there are the carnations, pinks, sweet peas, dahlias and the few chickens and turkeys that are reared for Christmas to be picked, nourished and cared for.

Like so many other Cornishmen I have spoken to, Nigel has two sons who wish to carry on with their father's work. But Nigel told me that they are facing harder times. 'We make the same amount of money that we did fifteen years ago and that can't be a good thing when the cost of everything has risen so much.'

It will be a sad day indeed if flower growing in the Tamar Valley disappears.

Already many of the slopes that were once covered in flowers are now planted out with evergreen trees and just here and there in between the trees you can see the strips of daffodils still flowering as if to remind us of times past. Since these daffodils are no longer picked they are a marvellous sight when they come into full bloom and the hillside is covered in white and yellow during the early spring.

Another sight I like to imagine in this part of the world is that of men ploughing and working with horses amongst the flowers and the cherry trees. At Crocadon Farm, once the manor house of the Coryton

'It is the patterns traced by the strip cultivation across the steep slopes that lend the Tamar Valley much of its character and beauty.'

Kit Hill Quarry above the Tamar Valley: '... now left in silence with the bottomless pool reflecting the chiselled walls around.'

Wintry woods

family who later moved to Pentillie Castle, Ron Martin once worked with horses. He told me the story of ploughing in the fields during the early years of the second world war and stopping one afternoon to gaze at some aeroplanes flying low over the valley in the direction of Plymouth. It was only later that he discovered their errand of destruction, for this was the city's first terrible air-raid.

Ron Martin has turned his hand to many different kinds of agriculture in the Tamar Valley. He has worked with the fruit-growers when gooseberries, strawberries, raspberries, currants and cherries were produced in abundance. He has also worked with vegetables and flowers. But what he seems to remember with greatest pleasure is 'a good day behind a nice pair of horses'.

His day with the horses would start at seven in the morning when he would feed and groom the animals and then start out into the fields at eight taking with him a bit of 'crib' to be eaten at ten. 'We had a quarter of an hour for crib and we took with us bottles of tea wrapped up in stockings to keep them warm.' At twelve they would stop for a more substantial meal of pasties and sandwiches. 'The boss would always give us some cider when we were working at Crocadon,' Ron told me.

'You would cover quite a few miles when you were ploughing,' Ron said. At five in the evening the busy day would be over and time to dry down the horses, feed them and groom them.

Although his life was tough he remembers it with happiness even on wet Cornish days when it 'was raining streams'. He had no holidays, was paid what would be considered a pittance nowadays and felt privileged to have Boxing Day off. Of the young he says, 'They are spoon fed these days, with silver spoons.'

When anyone needs a helping hand to this day Ron is there. He can build a dry stone wall with expertise, milk cows, cut the docks and thistles in the fields, walk for miles beating for the shooting parties and in his retirement is as busy as he ever was. He has only recently got used to the fact that he does not have to rise with the birds, but can choose his time as he pleases.

His life may have taken place in a small and protected area but he has seen so many changes, has taken part in so many different activities, that it has been far fuller and probably more rewarding and interesting than many a town-dweller or jet-set traveller.

He came from a large family who lived at Calstock. His father worked on the barges transporting bricks and coal and so their lives were affected by the building of the Calstock viaduct which eventually put a stop to the river traffic.

Changes he has seen; a different world has grown up around him; the river traffic and much of the fruit and vegetable growing have disappeared. The sight of horses working the fields has quite gone. It must be a totally different landscape to people like Ron Martin. But though he may, from time to time, mention a little regret for times past, he is as content and active as ever, and seemingly full of happy memories.

The Author at Trematon Castle, near Saltash in the Tamar Valley, during the time her parents lived there.

VIEWS OF OLD CORNWALL
by Sarah Foot.
Nearly 200 old picture postcards from the Peter Dryden collection, with text by Sarah Foot, all combine to recall Cornwall as she once was.
'… will be certain to start the talk flowing of days gone by.'
The Cornishman

A CORNISH CAMERA
by George Ellis and Sarah Foot.
More than 200 photographs taken by George Ellis, the doyen of Cornish press photographers: Cornwall at work and play in war and peace; town and countryside and coast; personalities and customs; triumphs and tragedies. Sarah Foot's text adds the stories behind these pictures.
'A delightful nostalgic look back at the last 40 years in the County.'
Sunday Independent
'An elegant book … its fascinating photographs fix Cornwall to the page like nothing else could.'
Tom Salmon BBC Radio

THE CORNISH YEAR BOOK
Over 150 photographs and drawings.
Writers, artists and photographers have all combined to reveal facets of Cornwall and a Cornish way of life through spring, summer, autumn and winter.

AROUND LAND'S END
Michael Williams explores the end and the beginning of Cornwall. Wrecks and legends, the Minack Theatre, Cable & Wireless, Penwith characters and customs, lighthouses and Lyonesse all feature. 90 photographs, many of them from Edwardian and Victorian times, help to tell the story.

THE CALL OF THE WEST
by Arthur Caddick
Selected lyric poems with a comic interlude.
'This book is as delightful as the reader can hope. The landscape, the seasons, the people, the history. Mr Caddick dips his lyric, his comic, his emotional pen — in turn — into the ink of life.'
The Cornishman
'It's my belief that Arthur Caddick is the Dylan Thomas of Cornwall. Like Dylan Thomas he has the gift of touching our hearts.'
Derek Tangye

VIEWS OF OLD PLYMOUTH
by Sarah Foot.
Words and old pictures combine to recall Plymouth as it once was: a reminder of those great times past and of the spirit of the people of Plymouth.
'This is a lovely nostalgia-ridden book and one which no real Plymothian will want to be without.'
James Mildren, The Western Morning News

FOLLOWING THE TAMAR
by Sarah Foot. 63 photographs and map.
Sarah Foot is the Tamar's inevitable author, living only a mile from its banks, seeing it every day from her Cornish home, and truly loving it.
'…both a labour of love and a work of subtle selection, combining the intriguing byways of local history and geography with a profusion of well-chosen black and white plates.'
Dick Benson-Gyles, The Western Evening Herald

FOLLOWING THE RIVER FOWEY
by Sarah Foot. 49 photographs.
Sarah Foot follows the Fowey from its beginnings on Bodmin Moor to where it meets the sea beyond Fowey and Polruan. 'She stitches into the simple tapestry of the river's story names and incidents and anecdotes, deftly and lovingly, every thread and every page touched with charm and an unashamed sense of delight.'
Western Morning News

LEGENDS OF CORNWALL
by Sally Jones. 60 photographs and drawings.
Brilliantly illustrated with photographs and vivid drawings of legendary characters. A journey through the legendary sites of Cornwall, beginning at the Tamar and ending at Land's End.
'Highly readable and beautifully romantic …'
Desmond Lyons, Cornwall Courier

GHOSTS OF CORNWALL
by Peter Underwood. 41 drawings and photographs.
Peter Underwood, President of the Ghost Club, journeys across haunted Cornwall. Photographs of haunted sites and drawings of ghostly characters all combine to prove that Cornwall is indeed a mystic land.

We shall be pleased to send you our catalogue giving full details of our growing list of titles for Devon and Cornwall and forthcoming publications.

If you have difficulty in obtaining our titles, write direct to Bossiney Books, Land's End, St Teath, Bodmin, Cornwall.